GW00470791

A COMPLETE GUIDE
TO
THE ISLE OF WIGHT

BEAUTIFUL WORLD ESCAPES

WWW.BEAUTIFULWORLDESCAPES.COM

TABLE OF CONTENTS

Introduction

For the last 150 years, the Isle of Wight has enjoyed a reputation for being the most popular seaside destination in the United Kingdom. It also boasts the most tourist attractions per square mile in the country, making it wonderful for tourists who like plenty of things to see and do.

Some of the biggest attractions on the Isle of Wight, such as Carisbrooke Castle and Osborne House, showcase the island's intricate and rich history. The oldest theme park, Blackgang Chine, can be found here, dating back well over 150 years ago.

The island is also renowned for its rugged natural beauty, with its unique environment attractive whether it's raining or sunny. With long stretches of National Trust coastline that remain unspoilt to animal sanctuaries and stunning parks, the entire family will be amused.

For history lovers, the Isle of Wight is guaranteed to peak your interest. There are multiple historic attractions ranging from various periods; Dinosaur Isle is ideal for those interested in palaeontology and fossils, Brading Roman Villa gives you an insight into life here during the Roman period, and Carisbrooke Castle, where King Charles I stayed during his confinement. With many more attractions, history certainly comes to life.

It was from the Victorian era that the Isle of Wight began to really start attracting visitors, including a wealth of artists that found inspiration from the beautiful countryside and rugged coastline. From Keates to Tenneyson, to a variety of contemporary painters, sculptors, poets, and many others, it had resulted in a thriving artistic scene, ideal for those who like to bring something back from their travels.

Chapter One – Practicalities

Getting to the Isle of Wight

By Air

The closest airport to the Isle of Wight is Bournemouth International Airport (BOH), located in the mainland at Bournemouth City, which accepts both domestic and international flights. However, many international visitors tend to arrive at London Heathrow Airport (LHR) or Gatwick Airport (LGW). Bournemouth Airport is located around 20 minutes away from the harbour where visitors embark on a boat to cross the water to the island, whereas Gatwick Airport is one hour 23 minutes, and Heathrow Airport an hour and 12 minutes away.

All airports have great transportation links to the several ports where you can board a boat to the Isle of Wight, the most popular places being Bournemouth and Portsmouth.

By Train

There are frequent trains from London that travel straight to the Isle of Wight, with London Waterloo and London Victoria being the most popular starting points. Both of which offer fast and regular trains via Southampton and Portsmouth Harbour.

At Portsmouth Harbour, you have the choice to take the Fast Cat service by Wightlink to Ryde, or to Fishbourne from Gunwharf Quays. The hovercraft is extremely popular; you can catch this from Portsmouth and Southsea station or from the other terminal at Southsea.

From Southampton Central, the Red Funnel service arrives in both Cowes and East Cowes, taking just over an hour to reach both destinations.

By Car

Depending on your starting point, there are several routes to reach the Isle of Wight, the two main ones being the A3 and the M3, which can be accessed from the M25. The M3 is better for those coming from Southampton or Lyimington, but for those from southern England will most likely take the A3.

By Coach

The National Express is the biggest coach company in the UK and offers regular journeys from numerous cities, towns, and airports to Portsmouth, Southsea, and Southampton which are timed so that passengers can access services to the Isle of Wight. There are many deals on the National Express website where they offer deals on combined coach and crossing journeys, as well as accommodation and attractions.

Getting Around the Isle of Wight

By Bus

Southern Vectis is the local bus services which provides a good network and coverage over the island. Many of the bus routes are designed to stop outside or close to many of the attractions.

By Train

The trains on the Isle of Wight are limited but are a good, easy way of exploring the many sights. The trains are over 80 years old, originally used during the London Underground tube service during the 1930s. The Isle of Wight Steam Railway is an attraction all by itself and is connected with the main train service, covering five miles from Havenstreet to Ashley.

Climate

The Isle of Wight has one of the best records for sunshine in the United Kingdom. Even though the island is just 150 square miles, the temperature and weather can vary from place to place. March is generally the coldest month, when temperatures can drop down to 4°C, with August being the hottest month of the year, with temperatures as high as 21°C. The rainiest time of the year is in January. With such drastic changes in the weather, visitors are urged to pack accordingly. During the winter months, a warm waterproof proof and gloves are essential. During the rest of the months, a light jacket, sunglasses, and a hat is useful. Umbrellas should be carried throughout the year.

Currency

The currency used in the United Kingdom is the British Pound (GBP) and the currency symbol used is £. Foreign currency can be exchanged at various travel agencies, banks, and currency converter booths which can be found throughout the various towns and cities within the country.

Chapter Two – Attractions

Bembridge Windmill

Located at Bembridge, this is the last windmill on the Isle of Wight to survive. It is a Grade One listed building and is one of the top attractions on the island. It dates from around the turn of the 18th century and ceased to be used in 1913, although much of the machinery inside is still intact. Visitors can climb to the top and enjoy panoramic views over the area and learn how it was used over the years. Various hiking and nature trails in the area are ideal for those who like to enjoy the outdoors.

Address: Mill Road, Bembridge, Isle of Wight, PO35 5SQ.

The Needles Old Battery

Located above the Needles on the very apex of the island, sits the Needles Old Battery, a fort dating to the Victorian period which was used through World Wars I and II. The fort was constructed in 1862 and its history can be traced through a range of iconic objects displayed in several rooms, including the cartoons Geoff Campion, the famous comic book artist, illustrated. Outside, the site includes two original guns and a subterranean tunnel which takes you to a searchlight emplacement where the views over the Needles are extraordinary.

Head a little further up to visit the New Battery, where the underground rooms feature beautiful exhibits of the UK's race to create rockets under a blanket of secrecy.

Address: West High Down, Alum Bay, Isle of Wight, PO39 0JH.

Freshwater

Freshwater boasts the vibrancy of a large town but is quiet and small enough to be classed as a village. Popular with visitors who head to the beautiful sandy Freshwater Bay, the village enjoys a variety of shops, accommodation, restaurants, a sports centre and an 18-hole golf course that boasts incredible views. Over the years, Freshwater has been the home to many celebrities, including Alfred Lord Tennyson and Julia Margaret Cameron.

The Isle of Wight Shipwreck Centre and Maritime Museum

A vast range of objects and artefacts are arranged in well-laid out displays at this small museum in Arreton. For children, the museum holds a little treasure hunt which, at the end, they are awarded with their own treasure.

Address: Arreton.

The Classic Boat Museum

Located in East Cowes, the Classic Boat Museum boasts an excellent collection of classic boats and sailing memborilia, ideal for both adults and children alike.

Address: Albany Road, East Cowes PO32 6AA.

Niton

Not far from Ventnor, Niton is a pleasant little village that features several churches, a range of shops, and a pottery workshop. The lower section of the village, which sits underneath the cliff, is referred to as the Undercliff, that was a magnificently charming fishing hamlet during the 19th century. Some of the biggest attractions in and around the area include St. Catherine's lighthouse and St. Catherine's Point.

Dinosaur Isle

Located in Sandown, Dinosaur Isle was the UK's first dinosaur museum and attraction to be established. The Isle of Wight is famous for its plentiful fossils that give us great insight into the history of the region millions of years ago as well as the possible environmental changes in the future. The rocks here give us information up to 126 million years ago, making it one of the best places in Europe for dinosaur material. The younger rocks provide records of the various animals that lived, not just on the island itself, but in the skies and seas surrounding it. The youngest fossils date to the more recent Ice Ages.

The museum offers a variety of displays that takes visitors on a fascinating journey through millions of years of history, as well as offering guided walks around the area, bringing the history of the dinosaurs to life.

Address: Culver Parade, Sandown, Isle of Wight, PO36 8QA.

Calbourne Watermill

Calbourne Watermill, located in 35 acres of stunning countryside just outside the village of Calbourne Village, is the only working watermill on the island. It takes its name after the village, which in turn is named after the bourne, or stream, which the mill is powered by.

The watermill dates back to the 11th century, when it was first mentioned in the Doomsday Book along with a second mill; together, these mills were worth 6s 3d. Using traditional methods, Calbourne Watermill still produces up to 40 tonnes of flour each day.

There are plenty of things to experience in the area surrounding the mill. Young children will enjoy feeding the ducks, geese, peacocks and other birds, as well as exploring the beauty of the ancient woodland, home to a variety of animals, including foxes, red squirrels, and badgers. Located at the base of the hill, the steam is home to many eels which are captivating to watch. Visitors can also feed the fish in the stream by the mill – these fish are so large that they tend to almost jump out of the water to take the food from your hands. Head back up the hill to enjoy spectacular views over the countryside.

Other attractions close by include a war museum, an adventure golf course, punting down the stream, and many cafes serving homemade dishes and cakes.

Address: Newport Road, Calbourne, PO30 4JN.

Brading Town

Brading Town may be one of the smallest towns on the island but it is one of the oldest and most charming. The High Street is steeped in history and appeal, with the Bull Ring located in the heart of the town, along with St. Mary's Church, dating back to the Norman period, and the Old Town Hall, complete with the whipping post and stocks. Other attractions in and around the town include Nunwell House and the world-famous Brading Roman Villa.

Liliput Museum of Antique Dolls and Toys

Located within Brading Town, the Liliput Museum of Antique Dolls and Toys is a speciality museum that showcases a vast range of toys from the last 200 years. This is a great way of modern children learning what previous generations played with and for adults of all ages to take a trip down memory lane.

Address: High Street, Brading PO36 0DJ.

Butterfly World and Fountain World

Anyone interested in butterflies will enjoy visiting Butterfly World, home to hundreds of the beautiful creatures. Visitors are given the opportunity to see butterflies of many species fly free in a natural environment, enabling you to see first-hand the life cycle they go through. Fountain World and a beautiful koi pond make for tranquil spots to sit quietly and reflect on the world.

Address: Staplers Road, Wootton Bridge PO33 4RW.

Newport

Newport is one of the most popular towns on the Isle of Wight. Located in the centre of the island, it is a busy and energetic town with many shops, boutiques, supermarkets, cinemas, theatres, art centres, restaurants, cafes, pubs, and many other amenities. With a variety of family-oriented attractions such as Robin Hill Adventure Park and Monkey Haven situated close by, there is also something to keep you busy here.

Yarmouth

Positioned along the north coastline on the Western Yar River estuary, Yarmouth is definitely a highlight of any trip to the island. Overlooking the harbour town like a mother protecting her flock is Yarmouth Castle, which dates back to the 16th century, created to safeguard the town from invaders. Yarmouth Pier is a great spot for fishing, whilst the town boasts a number of excellent restaurants, pubs, and shops. The harbour has a car ferry service to Lymington in the New Forest.

Osborne House

Osbourne House is perhaps one of the best-known attractions on the island. After her first visit to the Isle of Wight, Queen Victoria said, *"It is impossible to imagine a prettier spot"*. She would go on to visit the island regularly, staying at Osbourne House with her husband, Prince Albert, and their nine children.

Visitors to Osbourne House can enjoy a tantalising insight into the life and family of Queen Victoria, with tours around the Royal Apartments, the Durbar Room (inspired by India), and the nurseries of the royal children featuring original furniture and artwork.

Head outside and explore the vast grounds. The gardens are beautifully maintained and the views across the Solent are claimed to remind Prince Albert of the Bay of Naples. Recently, the private beach used by the royals is now open to the public.

Address: York Avenue, East Cowes, PO32 6JX.

Bembridge and Seaview Villages

Situated on the eastern tips of the island, the small coastal villages of Bembridge and Seaview are exquisitely charming and steeped in history. Their small beaches are ideal for families with children who like to explore rock pools, swimming and sunbathing. There is a small but vibrant harbour in Bembridge, inundated with dinghy's, boats, and house boats on one side. The villages are quaint and traditional, with a good range of stores to browse along with a selection of cafes, restaurants, and pubs.

Quarr Abbey

The ruins of Quarr Abbey dates to 1132 and remained an important part of local spiritual life until Henry VIII ordered the destruction of all the abbeys in the country. A new abbey was constructed adjacent to the ruins and belongs to the Solesmes Congregation, with the first monks arriving in 1907. Guided tours are available on the first Tuesdays of the month and every

Tuesdays during July and August, where guides take you through the pilgrim chapel and the church, providing a unique insight into the architecture, the local community, Saint Benedict, and the day-to-day routines of the monks who serve the abbey.

Enjoy a drink or something to eat at the Quarr Abbey Tea and Farm Shop, which uses fair-trade ingredients and organically grown produce on site and serves homemade cakes, lunches and meals.

Address: Quarr Road, Ryde, PO33 4ES.

Whitwell

Located in the south of the island, Whitwell is a charming village around five kilometres from Ventnor. This village has a strong sense of community and boasts a 700-year-old church, the oldest pub on the Isle of Wight dating back to the 15th century, and the famous White Well from which the village takes its name. Every year, the villagers will dress it up during the summer in honour of those who made their way here during the Medieval period on pilgrimages to the Holy Land.

The National Poo Museum

Founded by Dave Badman, Nigel George, and Daniel Roberts in joint efforts with the Isle of Wight Zoo, the National Poo Museum opened on the 25th March 2016. Inside are displays of poo from various animals, including lion, elk, baby humans, and a 140-million-year old fossil poo. It was established to further our knowledge on the substance that every creature creates and to remove the stigma surrounding it, along with highlighting the lack of sanitation in third-world countries.

Address: Yaverland Road, Sandown, PO36 8QB.

The IW Steam Railway

To recapture the magic of bygone eras, take a trip on the Isle of Wight Steam Railway. It goes through five miles of untainted countryside via Wootton, Havenstreet, Ashey, and Smallbrook, captivating the imagination when steaming past. Steam locomotives and wooden carriages continued to be used on the island between the 19th and mid-20th century, until they were replaced by more modern trains from the mainland. However, the steam trains were excellently preserved and remained an iconic part of local culture.

Passengers on the old steam trains can enjoy fantastic views over the countryside dotted with original old railway buildings which have been expertly restored. It has been used in countless television shows, documentaries, and films, and has won several impressive awards.

Address: Havenstreet, Ryde, PO33 4DS.

Brading Roman Villa

Brading Roman Villa is perhaps one of the best preserved British-Romano villas in the country. There have been several constructions projects on the site, but the earliest structure dates back to the mid-first century but wasn't discovered until 1879 when Mr Munns, a local sheep farmer, stumbled across mosaic floors when digging post holes. This started a series of excavations which eventually uncovered a magnificent villa. A dozen rooms have been discovered, five of which feature mosaic floors; the style and quality of these suggests that the original owners were both prosperous and powerful.

Explore the ancient mosaics, before heading up to the modern Visitor Centre and Museum where you can understand more about the significance of the site.

Address: Morton Old Road, Brading, PO36 0PH.

Hollier's Park

Located in the charming Arreton Valley, Hollier's Park and House of Chili blend traditional arts and crafts along with delicious local food. The main building was fashioned by agricultural polytunnels and feature a wide range of food and drinks from all over the island, including honey, jams, and ales. A variety of luxury hampers are also on offer, starting from £20, giving you a wonderful taste of the Isle of Wight.

House of Chili features products and dishes that uses the spicy ingredient. The Ghost Chili Peanut Butter is an iconic food item on offer, but for those who think they can handle the hottest of chilis, then then Psycho Juice 70% Scorpion Pepper will certainly have you reaching for a glass of water or two.

Address: Holliers Farm, Branstone, PO36 0LT.

The Depozitory

The Depozitory, located in Ryde, was the former chapel of the 19th century Wesleyn movement, better known as the Methodists. Many chapels were created around the island for the followers; the one you see here today dates back to around 1832. Inside the building is an interesting exhibition on the architecture and history of the building, including the period when it was deconsecrated and transformed into a warehouse during the latter part of World War I. In 2000, the building was purchased and lovingly renovated. Today, it is used for cultural and art exhibitions throughout the year, as well as for the arts festival held annually in July.

Address: 23 Nelson Street, Ryde, Isle of Wight, PO33 2EZ.

Arreton Barns

Arreton Barns is an arts and craft village, free from traffic, that has been the heart of the island for over a thousand years. Skilled artisans open their studios every day to the public, where visitors can learn more about the traditional crafts, from leather to glasswork, from wood turners to painters.

After exploring the beautiful products on display, visitors can wander around the village. Attractions include the Church of St. George, dating to the 12th century and features the world-renowned Burma Star window, and the Dairyman's Daughter, a traditional pub named after Elizabeth Wallbridge, who died in 1801. She was featured in the *Annals of the Poor* and is buried in the nearby graveyard.

Address: Main Road, Arreton, Isle of Wight, PO30 3AA.

Dimbola Lodge

Located in Freshwater Bay, Dimbola Lodge was the former residence of Julia Margaret Cameron, a Victorian photographer. Her home was transformed into a gallery and museum that showcases her amazing work and life, as well as showcasing works from contemporary photographers.

Address: Terrace Lane, Freshwater Bay, PO40 9QE.

Quay Arts Centre

Located at the top of the River Medina in Newport, the Quay Arts Centre was opened in 1997 and features three galleries, theatre, gift shop, and café bar. Housed in a 19th century brewery warehouse, it has gained a reputation for some of the best visual arts exhibitions, showcasing work from local and international artists.

Address: 15 Sea Street, Newport Harbour, PO30 5BD.

Chessell Pottery Barns

Chessell Pottery Barns is a popular pottery studio where visitors can come and create a souvenir to take back home, as well as recording baby hand and footprints. Visitors can choose from a wide variety of earthenware or exclusive Emma Bridgewater pottery before starting to paint. Help is always available from the staff and if you cannot collect it before the end of your trip, the studio can arrange for it to be sent home for you.

Address: Brook Road, Yarmouth, PO41 0UE.

Los Altos Park

West of Sandown is Los Altos, a large park ideal for lazy days when you are looking for charm and relaxation. The path that leads from the south of Sandown railway station winds through a thick canopy of trees and bypasses several facilities and amenities, including an exercise area.

Address: Melville Street, Sandown, PO36 9DH.

Ventnor Botanic Garden

Located in the centre of the Undercliff and protected against the fierce winds by the chalk downs, Ventnor Botanic Garden is a stunning garden renowned for its subtropical plant collections that are grown outside. Spread out over several sections that are based on geographical locations, visitors can enjoy learning about some of the various plants grown around the world.

Address: Undercliff Drive, Ventnor, PO38 1UL.

Mottistone Manor

Located in Mottistone Village, Mottistone Manor is a National Trust property and a listed building. Its history stretches back over a thousand years ago, being first mentioned in various documents that were linked to the Domesday Book which was compiled in 1086. The south-east manor is the oldest part of the building, dating to the 15th century, with the north-west wing remodelled in 1567 by Thomas Cheke. The manor also saw new additions added in the 17th century. In the early 20th century, it underwent several restorations.

Go for a stroll around the gardens; the rose garden makes for a truly romantic experience and the wild herb garden is fragrant with various scents of different herbs. There are several paths that wind up the hill, dotted with benches for visitors to enjoy panoramic views over the garden, the village, and the sea.

Address: Mottistone, near Brighstone, PO30 4EA.

Shanklin Chine

Shaklin Chine is a stunningly beautiful gorge formed over thousands of years and lined with ancient trees, stretching from Shaklin Old Village all the way to the beach. Visitors can explore its beauty by day and enjoy the magic of it at night, when the countless lights along the pathways illuminate the streams and waterfalls.

The nearby Heritage Centre provides highly interesting exhibitions on World War II, art, photography, and the PLUTO exhibition. Fisherman's Cottage is located on the beach below Shanklin Chine, constructed in 1817 by William Colenutt.

Address: 3 Chine Hill, Shanklin, Isle of Wight, PO37 6BW.

Battery Gardens

Located in Sandown, Battery Gardens are the fortifications used to protect the country from invasion during World War II that were transformed into serene gardens. With outstanding views over the English Channel, this small but charming park is along the path that runs along the cliffs connecting Sandown with Shanklin. A children's play area is situated amongst the beautiful trees and flowers.

Address: Talbot Road, Sandown, PO36 8NP.

Blackgang Chine

Blackgang Chine is the oldest theme park in the country. Located just outside Ventnor and overlooking the English Channel, both adults and children alike will discover thrills and magic in one place. Children can become a princess in Fairytown, or sail the seven seas in Pirate Cove, run away from dinosaurs in Dinosaurland, and enjoy a variety of thrilling rides for all ages.

Address: Blackgang, Ventnor PO38 2HN.

Robin Hill

Robin Hill, which also runs Blackgang Chine, is one of the top attractions on the Isle of Wight. Situated in 88 acres of stunning countryside, it is a fantastic theme park and gardens ideal for the entire family. There are numerous rides, an adventure play area, ponds, gardens, walking trails, and a falconry show. At the weekend, the park also hosts the popular Saturday Night at the Movies attraction, where visitors can enjoy a range of movies in the woodland amphitheatre.

Address: Downend, Newport, PO30 2NU.

Godshill Model Village

Godshall Model Village is located in the Old Vicarage and was first introduced to the public in 1952. The models of Shanklin were created by Mr. Dams in order to fill up the upper part of the gardens. In the bottom half are stunning models of Godshill which were created by Robin Thwaites along with model artists from Pinewood Studios.

Address: High Street, Godshill, PO38 3HH.

Tapnell Farm

Tapnell Farm is a fun action-packed attraction for the entire family. The farm is home to a wide range of animals, including rare and exotic creatures such as meerkats and wallabies. In the Big Animal Farm, visitors can learn more about different animals before petting some. The Big Paddock is home to some of the larger breeds, and the Wallaby Walkabout is where you can find the rarer species.

There are plenty of things for everyone to do at the farm; the Play Barn features an extensive soft play area, the Imagination

Playground, a climbing wall and many other activities. Go zip wiring or enjoy a few laps around the indoor and outdoor pedal go kart tracks in the Straw Barn. An outdoor play area which includes a large jumping pillow will burn off any excess energy. To refuel, enjoy a light meal at the Farm Park Café or the Cow Co. Restaurant.

Address: Newport Road, Yarmouth, Isle of Wight, PO41 0YJ.

Shanklin Seafront

Shanklin Seafront is one of the most popular beaches on the island, featuring a range of amenities, including three crazy golf courses, an amusement arcade, ten-pin bowling, go karts, café, and an indoor play area for children.

Address: Shanklin Esplanade, Shanklin, PO37 6BG.

Bembridge Beaches

A delightfully beautiful rocky and sandy beach overlooking the Solent, visitors can enjoy watching ships go sailing past, exploring the rock pools with children, or looking for cockles to eat. The beaches at Bembridge are typically quieter than others around the island, an ideal place for walking dogs, but the harbour is not safe for swimming.

Address: Bembridge, Isle of Wight.

Brook Beach

Brook Beach stretches for over a mile, and is popular with both fossil hunters and surfers. Underneath the cliffs at one end is a fossilised forest which appears when the tides are low enough. Dogs are welcome all year round, and whilst the waters ae safe for swimming, there are some rocky areas.

Address: Brook, Isle of Wight.

Sandown Pier

Sandown Pier is an ideal destination for the entire family no matter what time of year you visit. There are plenty of activities to keep both children and adults busy, including an indoor golf course, ten pin bowling, a play area, a small amusement park area, cafes, ice cream kiosks, and a sports bar where you can enjoy beautiful views over the sea.

Address: Esplanade, Sandown, PO36 8JT.

Newchurch

Situated between Newport and Sandown on the southeast part of the island lies the town of Newchurch. It takes its name from the new church that was established here by the Norman monks of Lyra in 1987. For centuries, Newchurch was the biggest parish on the island and until the early 19th century, when Ventnor and Ryde started to increase in size. Today, the two other resorts are now not part of the parish but other villages that are included in Newchurch's boundaries includes Alverstone, Whiteley Bank, Winford, and Apse Heath. Major attractions in and around Newchurch include the Amazon World Zoo and the Garlic Farm.

West Wight Alpacas

In 2010, Michelle and Neil Payne opened West Wight Alpacas, a farm in Wellow that specialises in breeding alpacas and llamas, offering custom treks on the island for visitors. Starting with just eleven alpacas, the farm is now home to around 70 alpacas, 12 llamas, and a variety of other animals. Visitors can learn more about these magnificent creatures, how to use their fleece for a range of goods, and enjoy a unique trek across the island on their backs.

Address: Main Road, Wellow, PO41 0SZ.

Haven Falconry

Located in Havenstreet, Haven falconry is home to a large number of birds of prey, including falcons, owls, hawks, eagles and vultures, handled by skilled falconers. The goal of Haven Falconry is to further the knowledge and plight of many of these creatures, as well as preserving the traditional art of falconry itself. Conservation is at the heart of this establishment, especially with the Barn Owl, whose numbers are sadly dwindling in the British wild.

Visitors can enjoy getting to know these magnificent birds and enjoy a range of intriguing talks and displays of falconry. Private and smaller group experiences can be arranged for you to enjoy a close-up experience with these birds. Several specialised areas have been established for younger children, including the Pets Corner, Ferret Skywalk, and Insect Hotel.

Address: Main Road, Havenstreet, PO33 4DR.

Isle of Wight Zoo

Located in Sandown, the Isle of Wight Zoo was established within the ruins of a Victorian Fort that was once used to defend the island. Today, it is a world-famous zoo once known for walking tiger cubs along the beach, although today the zoo is more famous for giving a home to older tigers who are enjoying their retirement.

The Isle of Wight Zoo is dedicated to education, conservation, and care of all animals, with an emphasis on conservation. Many of the species that are housed in the zoo face severe problems in the wild due to human activity. The zoo regularly supports and funds conservation projects in Madagascar and India, as well as participating in breeding programs to ensure the continuation of several species originally from Madagascar.

Visitors can enjoy getting to know more about the various animals here, with a variety of informative talks and presentations.

Address: Yaverland Seafront, Sandown, PO36 8QB.

Amazon World Zoo Park

The Isle of Wight is famous for its great animal attractions and Amazon World is no exception. Dedicated to the conservation of the rainforests, the park is home to a wide variety of unusual and endangered animals that originate in the Amazon, some of which cannot be found within other European zoos. With crocodiles swimming in the ponds, tropical birds flying overhead, lemurs sunbathing and playing in front of you, Amazon World Zoo Park is a magical and informative place to bring the entire family.

Address: Watery Lane, Arreton, PO36 0LX.

Monkey Haven

Opened to the public in 2010, Monkey Haven offers a safe and secure home to primates and birds of prey who have found themselves in need of love and care. Some have been rescued from the illegal pet trade, some were unable to meet the specifications of certain breeding programs, and others have been bullied within their original groups or could not survive in the wild. Therefore, they find a new home at Monkey Haven where they are given a second chance at a good life. The facility provides interesting talks about the care and lifestyles of the animals here, and conservation efforts throughout the world.

Address: 5 Acres Farm, Staplers Road, Newport, PO30 2NB.

Donkey Sanctuary

Located in Wroxall, the Donkey Sanctuary offers a warm and loving home to nearly 100 donkeys and 25 horses and ponies. Some have been cases of neglect, others have needed to find shelter here due to their owner's circumstances, but all are well-loved and cared for here. The sanctuary offers the public the chance to learn more about these beautiful and friendly animals and learn how they can help.

Address: Lower Winstone Farm, St Johns Road, Wroxall, PO38 3AA.

Collwell Bay

With stunning views of Hurst Castle and the Solent, Collwell Bay is an ideal destination for those who prefer their beaches quiet with a relaxing atmosphere. There are several facilities and amenities for all ages and disabilities, including toilets, boat hires, water sports and water safety zones so that sun-bathers can soak up the sun in quieter areas.

Address: Collwell Bay, Isle of Wight.

Compton Bay

Located between Brook and Freshwater Bay, Compton Bay is a stunning sandy beach popular with kite surfers, windsurfers, and surfers who take advantage of the strong waves and winds. It is also popular with those who like to hunt for the past, namely fossils millions of years old – when the tides are low enough, footprints of dinosaurs can be seen stamped in the rocks.

Address: Compton Bay, Isle of Wight.

Gurnard

Situated to the west of Cowes, Gunard is a charming resort ideal for watching ships sail to and from Southampton. A sailing club meets regularly here, hosting races and the small pebbly beach offers excellent views. Other facilities here include a café, inn, and toilets. There is a walkway that runs along the sea wall, that is ideal for disabled and prams to stroll between Gurnard and Cowes, with various other cafes and restaurants dotted along the way.

Address: Gurnard, Isle of Wight.

East Cowes Promenade

East Cowes is popular with visitors and locals alike, who come here to enjoy the promenade and the beautiful views stretching over the water. There are plenty of things to do here, including woodland walks and a children's play area, as well as only being a few minutes' walk away from many restaurants, pubs, cafes, and shops in the main town.

Address: East Cowes, Isle of Wight.

Freshwater Bay

Highly popular with families, Freshwater Bay features a small sandy and shingle beach overlooked by imposing cliffs on both sides. There are several cafes and toilet facilities here, as well as the Freshwater Bay Golf Course.

Address: Freshwater Bay.

Ryde

Ryde Beach can be found north of the town centre, easily accessible by public transport, on foot, or by car. The beach runs for six miles between Seaview and Ryde Pier, with a walkway stretching from Ryde to Puckpool, dotted with gardens, children's play areas, beach huts, cafes, restaurants, and Appley Tower. The Dotto Train offers a nice relaxing way to get back to town during the summer months and the lake gives you the chance to go boating and cool off from the sun. The long sandy beach is ideal for relaxing but parents should be aware of fast moving tides.

Address: Ryde Beach, Ryde, Isle of Wight.

St. Helens Beach

Looking across the Solent and the shipping lanes, St. Helen's Beach is known for its beautiful views and the abundant wildlife surrounding it. Let kids explore the rock pools when the tides are out, before enjoying the stunning natural beauty along the beach.

Address: St. Helen's, Isle of Wight.

Steephill Cove

Steephill Cove is a charming and hidden small cove between the Undercliff and Ventnor where traditional fisherman continues to fish for lobsters and crabs. The cove is only accessible on foot, making it a rather quiet area to enjoy a few hours to yourself or to go rock pooling with children.

Address: Steephill Cove, Ventnor, Isle of Wight, Ventnor PO38 1UG.

Sandown Beach

Sandown Beach is the most famous beach on the island. Holding the Water Quality Award since 1996 and holder of the prestigious Blue Flag award, Sandown Beach stretches from Shanklin to Yaverland, with glorious views in-between. Sandown

Pier is open throughout the year, featuring an amusement arcade, fishing facilities, pub and a café. In the area, visitors can enjoy a game of crazy golf, let the children run wild at the play area, or go skating; other things to do include White City, the Sandown Lawn Bowls Club, and the Brown's Golf Course.

Address: Sandown, Isle of Wight.

Seagrove Beach

Seagrove Beach is a timelessly classic family friendly beach located between Seaview and St. Helen's. Overlooking the eastern Solent, the waters surrounding the beach are clear and the rock pools will keep children entertained looking for starfish and other sea creatures. The beach is only accessibly on foot via Seaview Village, but the sandy beach and safe waters makes it the perfect place with young families.

Address: Seaview Village, Isle of Wight.

Shanklin Beach

Shanklin Beach is part of Sandown Beach and is renowned for its glorious stretch of soft golden sands and safe waters. There are plenty of facilities to enjoy here, from cafes, pubs, restaurants, an amusement arcade and a pitch and putt area. For those who are after something a bit more thrilling, there are various water sports on offer here as well.

Address: Shanklin, Isle of Wight.

Springvale Beach

Springvale Beach is a charming family-friendly beach that can be accessed on foot, by car, or by public transportation. It consists of both sand and pebbles, and the waters surrounding it are safe for swimming. It is generally overlooked by Sandown Beach and Shanklin Beach, making it a great destination to escape the summer crowds.

Address: Springvale Road, Seaview, Isle of Wight, PO34 5AR.

Totland Bay

Located on the west side of the island, Totland Bay is a pleasant beach popular with yachts and large boats. As Shanklin Beach and Sandown Beach are generally more popular with tourists, Totland Bay is relatively quiet, with pebbles at the top and golden sands close to the water's edge. There are several facilities and amenities to enjoy in the area, including restaurants, cafes, pubs, and a pier.

Address: Totland Bay, Isle of Wight.

Ventnor Beach

If you are searching for long stretches of golden sandy beach with beautiful views over the sea and surrounded by a variety of amenities and facilities, look no further than Ventnor Beach. There is a somewhat Mediterranean feel to the beach, just a short distance away from Ventnor Town and surrounded by countless cafes, restaurants, and pubs. With rock pools on one side and a boat haven on the other side, Ventnor Beach is the ideal destination for the entire family.

The Needles

The Needles are the most iconic image of the Isle of Wight, as well as one of the top rock formations to be photographed in the world. Consisting of three unique chalk stacks, the Needles are truly unforgettable.

They take their name from the thin elongated rock pinnacle that used to be positioned slightly north to where the rocks stand today. Known as Lot's Wife, the needle-like rock was around 120 feet high and then collapsed into the sea in 1764; when the tides are low enough, the base of it can still be seen.

The chalk rocks are part of a band that stretches from the heart of the island to Culver Cliff in the east before heading all the way to the Isle of Purbeck in Dorset underneath the sea. Scientists believe it used to be part of the Old Harry Rocks, located around 20 miles away; around 5,000 BCE, the Solent River ruptured it, which then formed the island.

Wright Karting

Get your adrenaline pumping at Wright karting, a fantastic go karting company located in Ryde. There are separate tracks for younger and older racers, with safety gear provided. Highly recommended for teenagers wanting a bit of excitement.

Address: Brading Road, Westridge, Ryde PO33 1QS.

Yaverland Beach

Yaverland Beach is a relatively quiet beach around a mile away from Sandown Beach; it is more popular with locals who like to get away from the crowded tourist resorts and those who like to walk their dogs. It's a great place for water sports and watching yachts sail past. There is a kiosk here and toilet facilities.

Address: Yaverland Road, Sandown PO36 8QB.

Binstead

Binstead was founded well over a thousand years ago; it was recorded in the Domesday Book as Benestede, where it was renowned for its limestone. The limestone industry that made it so popular can still be seen today in the landscape and the various places that takes their names from it. Quarry Abbey is one of these, taking its name from the word quarry. The village itself is a charming example of tradition British villages, with a good selection of shops and restaurants, as well as several great walking trails in and around the village and running along the northeast coastline.

St. Catherine's Lighthouse

The first light to warn passing ships of the nearby dangers that lurked close by was established on the island in 1323. St. Catherine's Lighthouse dates to a much later period, but has long been guiding the way for ships sailing in the English Channel and for those approaching the Solent. It sits on a steep hill and boasts an interesting exhibition and tour of the lighthouse. Climb to the top of it for amazing views over the coast.

Address: Niton, Isle of Wight.

Brighstone

Situated in along the southwest coastline, Brighstone is a parish that consists of several villages, including Brighstone, Limerstone, Mottistone, Hulverstone, and Brook. The coastline here is famous amongst scientists and is now classed as a site of special scientific interest due to the amazing palaeontological discoveries. Each of the villages are incredibly charming, but Brighstone is particularly popular as it is a conservation area boasting 85 buildings and structures as officially protected.

Yarmouth Castle

An English Heritage property, Yarmouth Castle is a relatively small castle compared to others in the country, but it is a good example of British castles at their best. It was constructed under the orders of Henry VIII in 1547 to defend the surrounding area from continental invasions and features a wonderful exhibition on the history of the town and the castle itself, including a short documentary for visitors to watch. The fortified gun platform, complete with original 16th century guns, is one of the highlights here and gives you incredible views over the water.

Address: Yarmouth Castle Quay Street, Yarmouth PO41 0PB.

Calbourne

Calbourne Parish, like Brighstone, consists of several villages, namely Porchfield, Newtown, and Calbourne, where visitors can enjoy the relaxed atmosphere and take in the sights. There are several things to see and do here, including Westover House, which used to belong to the family of renowned poet, Elizabeth Barrett. Other attractions here include Winkle Street and an old mill, with the original dating back to the late 13th century. The natural harbour at Newtown, which used to be called Francheville or Freetown, is operated by the National Trust.

Appuldurcombe House

Appuldurcombe House is a magnificent English Heritage property that is a prime example of what life was like on the island during the 18th century. The property is basically just a shell of its former glory, but it gives visitors a sense of the grandeur and prestige it held many years ago. Visitors can explore the house and learn more about the history – and scandals – that went on here.

Address: Appuldurcombe Road, Wroxall PO38 3EW.

Chale

Located on the southern coastline between Blackgang Chine and Whale Chine, Chale is a small parish that offers tantalising views over the West Wight. It is the unspoilt natural beauty of the area that draws visitors here, along with its designation as a heritage coast and a site of special scientific interest. For many years, royalty from all over Europe would stay at the Clarendon Hotel, now renamed the Wight Mouse Inn, which is located a short walk from the coastline.

St. Mildred's Church

Located in a charming little village, St. Mildred's Church is a beautiful historic church that provides an interesting history of the building, the local area, and the religious reforms on the island over the years. It is especially popular with historians and those interested in the royal family since St. Mildred's daughter, Princess Beatrice, was married here.

Address: Beatrice Avenue, Whippingham.

Isle of Wight Bus and Coach Museum

Buses have long been part of the iconic history of the isle of Wight; run by a dedicated staff who have a great passion for the buses, visitors will be enraptured with nostalgia of the past at this beautiful speciality museum.

Address: Park Road, The Bus Depot, Ryde PO33 2BE.

Shalfleet

Shalfleet is a small village named after the shallow stream that meanders its way up to Newtown Creek. Steeped in charm and tradition, the tiny village which boasts just one main street, is on the way from Yarmouth to Newport. Ideal for those who want to experience a quintessentially traditional British village, Shalfleet boasts a beautiful church dedicated to St. Michael the Archangel, and a mill that was used to produce the flour for local bakeries up until the early 20th century. If you are interested in learning more about the history of the area, there is a local archive project available.

Shorwell

Shorwell is a delightful town situated in-between Whale Chine, Rowborough Down, Billingham, and Yafford, and was one of the places that Queen Victoria liked to visit when on the island. The town itself is established around the St. Peter's Church and three manor houses that are all steeped in history. St. Peter's Church is highly popular with visitors, with beautiful depictions of St. Christopher's life; it underwent remodelling in 1440 although the north chapel was constructed during the 12th century.

Westcourt is one of the three manors, dating to around 1500; whilst Northcourt was constructed around 1615; Wolverton is the third manor and a Grade One listed building, dating to the latter part of the 16th century. For those who are interested in architecture and historic buildings, the parish boasts over 20 Grade Two listed buildings to view.

The Wight Military and Heritage Museum

The Wight Military and Heritage Museum is a new addition to the island, dedicated to developing and furthering our knowledge about the history of the military on the island. There are a number of great displays, including an army jeep for kids to sit in and other military vehicles. A genuine bomb disposal robot is one of the many highlights here, and since it's interactive, it is ideal for children who aren't that keen on museums.

Address: 490 Newport Road, Cowes PO31 8QU.

Fort Victoria Railway Model Railway

Ideal for those who are interested in model railways, this little speciality museum boasts a good number of trains to gaze at. With good displays, buttons to activate some of them, and informative staff, the Fort Victoria Railway Model Railway is well worth a visit.

Address: Fort Victoria Westhill Lane, Norton, Yarmouth PO41 0RR.

Wootton

Wootton Creek has been utilised since the Roman occupation; centuries later, the monks from Quarr Abbey established a fishery here. Some of the houses here are more than 250 years old, the oldest in the village. It is a quiet place to explore, and usually ignored by tourists, but gives you a taste of traditional olde worlde Britain.

Chapter Three – Shopping

The Isle of Wight has a good selection of shopping centres and speciality stores to browse from all over the island. The smaller villages boast a number of high street stores as well as independent stores where you can find something unique to take home with you.

The Garlic Farm

The Garlic Farm is one of the most famous speciality stores on the Isle of Wight, offering a wide variety of food products that uses the smelly but tasty little ingredient. Visitors can sample some of these goods or enjoy a full meal, before purchasing some as little treats to take back home.

Address: Mersley Farm, Mersley Lane, Newchurch, Sandown PO36 0NR.

Diamond Isle Glass

This charming workshop gives visitors the chance to see how various glass objects and artworks are created. The items on display are all for sale and you can even have them personalised and engraved.

Address: Main Road, Arreton PO30 3AA.

Oldeworlde Antiques Centre

This intriguing store boasts a wide variety of knickknacks and antiques dating from various periods.

Address: 3 High Street, Sandown PO36 8DA.

Godshill Craft Market

Held on a weekly basis in the village of Godshill, this craft market is your one-stop destination for anything arts or crafts based. All hand-made, they make for a wonderful keepsake for your time on the Isle of Wight.

Chapter Four – Local Cuisine and Restaurants

The Isle of Wight may only be a small island, but it features a large variety of food and drink for visitors to sample. Many restaurants source their ingredients from local producers, giving you a true taste of the island. Fine dining is available in many hotels, numerous pubs across the island have won awards for the delectable dishes, and there are plenty of cafes for the budget conscious.

Fine Dining

Thompson's. 11 Town Lane, Newport, PO30 1JU. T: ++ 44 1983 526118. Cuisine: British, European, Contemporary.

The Little Gloster. 31 Marsh Road, Gurnard PO31 8JQ. T: +44 1983 298776. Cuisine: British, Seafood, Contemporary.

The Royal Hotel Restaurant. Belgrave Road, Ventnor PO38 1JJ. T: +44 1983 852186. Cuisine: British, Seafood, Contemporary.

Isla's restaurant. The George Hotel, Quay Street, Yarmouth PO41 0PE. T: +44 1983 760331. Cuisine: British, European.

The Oyster Store. 30-32 Sun Hill 7, Cowes PO31 7HY. T: +44 1983 209453. Cuisine: Seafood, British.

Ocean Restaurant. Hambrough Road, Ventnor PO38 1SQ. T: +44 1983 856333. Cuisine: Seafood.

The Island Room. Priory Bay Hotel, Priory Croft Priory Road, Priory Drive, Seaview PO34 5BU. T: +44 1983 613146. Cuisine: British.

The Hermitage. Bourne Hall Hotel, 11 Luccombe Road, Shanklin PO37 6RR. T: +44 1983 862820. Cuisine: British.

Mid-Range

Burr's Restaurant. Lugley Street, Newport PO30 5HD. T: +44 1983 825470. Cuisine: British, European.

Keat's Cottage. 76 High Street, Shanklin PO37 6NJ. T: +44 1983 639661. Cuisine: British, Polish.

Mojac's Restaurant. 10A Shooters Hill, Isle of Wight, Cowes PO31 7BG. T: +44 1983 281118. Cuisine: British, European.

Ada Mediterranean Kitchen. 55 Union Street, Ryde PO33 2LG. T: +44 1983 564023. Cuisine: Mediterranean.

Bellamy's Bistro. 71 High Street, Sandown PO36 8AD. T: +44 1983 403288. Cuisine: British, European, Seafood.

Pointer Inn. High Street, Newchurch, Sandown PO36 0NN. T: +44 1983 865202. Cuisine: Pub, British.

Dan's Kitchen. Lower Green Road, St Helens PO33 1TS. T: ++ 44 1983 872303. Cuisine: British.

The Banstand. Culver Parade, Sandown PO36 8AT. T: +44 1983 406875. Cuisine: British.

Kynges Well. 10 High Street, Brading, Brading PO36 0DG. T: +44 1983 408776. Cuisine: British.

The Cow Co Restaurant. Newport Road, Tapnell Farm, Yarmouth PO41 0YJ. T: +44 1983 758725. Cuisine: Steakhouse, British.

Tramezzini. 14 High Street, Ventnor PO38 1RZ. T: +44 1983 855510. Cuisine: Mediterranean.

Michelangelo. 30 St. Thomas Street, Ryde PO33 2DL. T: +44 1983 811966. Cuisine: Italian.

The Old Thatch Tearooms. 4 Church Road, Shanklin PO37 6NU. T: +44 1983 865587. Cuisine: British.

Three Buoys. Appley Lane, Ryde PO33 1ND. T: +44 1983 811212. Cuisine: Seafood, European.

The Taverners. High Street, Godshill PO38 3HZ. T: +44 1983 840707. Cuisine: Pub, British.

Budget

The Happy Haddock. 87 High Street, Shanklin Old Village, Shanklin PO37 6NR. T: +44 1983 868570. Cuisine: British, Seafood.

Wonky Café. Peacock Hill, Bembridge PO35 5QB. T: +44 1983 872689. Cuisine: British, Café.

The Seapot. Wheelers Bay, Ventnor PO38 1HP. T: +44 1983 857787. Cuisine: Café, British.

Eegon's of Cowes. 72 High Street, Cowes PO31 7RE. T: +44 1983 291815. Cuisine: British, Café.

The Man in the Moon. 16-17 St. James Street, Newport PO30 5HB. T: +44 1983 530126. Cuisine: Pub, British.

Captain's Cabin. Colwell Chine Road, Colwell Bay, Freshwater PO40 9NP. T: +44 7768 448277. Cuisine: British, Café.

Hong Kong City. 112 Regent Street, Shanklin PO37 7AP. T: +44 1983 868878. Cuisine: Chinese.

Chia Wing. 3 Carisbrooke Road, Newport PO30 1BJ. T: +44 1983 528286. Cuisine: Chinese.

Mr T's Pizza Shed. 46 Atherley Road, Shanklin PO37 7AU. T: +44 1983 863361. Cuisine: Pizza, American.

Dalyan Shanklin. 28 High Street, Shanklin PO37 6JY. T: +44 1983 867471. Cuisine: Pizza, Turkish.

Chapter Five – Accommodation

The Isle of Wight offers a bountiful array of accommodation, ranging from five-star luxury hotels, family friendly bed and breakfasts, to campsites and holiday parks close to many of the resorts. Whether you're staying overnight or for much longer, this diverse range of accommodation ensures that there is always something suited for your tastes.

Five Stars

Hillside Hotel. 151 Mitchell Avenue, Ventnor PO38 1DR. T: 0191 580 2974.

The Hamborough. Hambrough Road, Ventnor PO38 1SQ.

Four Stars

Rowborough Hotel. 32 Arthurs Hill, Shanklin PO37 6EX. T: 01983 866072.

The Royal Hotel. Belgrave Road, Ventnor PO38 1JJ.

The Clifton. 1 Queens Road, Shanklin PO37 6AN. T: 01902 504315.

Lakeside Park Hotel and Spa. High Street, Wootton Bridge, Ryde PO33 4LJ.

Luccombe Hall Hotel. 8 Luccombe Road, Shanklin PO37 6RL. T: 01983 214113.

The Swiss Cottage Shanklin. 10 St. Georges Road, Shanklin PO37 6BA. T: 01902 504323.

The Wight. Avenue Road, Sandown PO36 8BN. 01983 214112.

The Chestnuts. 4 Hope Road, Shanklin PO37 6EA.

Caprera Hotel. 9 Melville Street, Sandown PO36 8LE.

Appley Hotel. 13 Queens Road, Shanklin PO37 6AW.

Freshwater Bay County House. Freshwater PO40 9RB.

Priory Bay Hotel. Priory Croft Priory Road, Seaview PO34 5BU.

Old Park Hotel. Old Park Road, Ventnor PO38 1XS.

St. George's House. 2 St. Georges Road, Shanklin PO37 6BA. T: 0191 580 3071.

Three Stars

Seaview Hotel. High Street, Seaview PO34 5EX. T: 01202 629371.

Premier Inn Isle of Wight Sandown. Newport Road, Merrie Gardens, PO36 9PE.

Bembridge Coast Hotel. Fishermans Walk, Bembridge PO35 5TH.

The Channel View Hotel. 24 Hope Road, Shanklin PO37 6EH. T: 0191 580 3038.

Wight Mouse Inn. Church Place, Chale PO38 2HA. T: 01983 220081.

Bay Broadway Park Hotel. Melville Street, Sandown PO36 9DJ. T: 0844 499 5710.

Melville Hall Hotel. Melville Street, Sandown PO36 9DH. T: 0191 580 3070.

Royal Esplanade Hotel. 16 Esplanade, Ryde PO33 2ED.

Trouville Hotel. 10-16 Esplanade, Sandown PO36 8LB.

Hotel Ryde Castle. Esplanade, Ryde PO33 1JA.

The George Hotel. Quay Street, Yarmouth PO41 0PE.

Rylstone Manor Hotel. 10 Popham Road, Shanklin PO37 6RG.

Villa Rothsay Hotel. 29 Baring Road, Cowes PO31 8DF.

Queensmead Hotel. 12 Queens Road, Shanklin PO37 6AN.

Cliff Hall Hotel. 16 Crescent Road, Shanklin PO37 6DJ.

The Wheatsheaf Hotel. 16 St. Thomas Square, Newport PO30 1SG.

Bourne Hall Country Hotel. 11 Luccombe Road, Shanklin PO37 6RR.

Marlborough Hotel. 16 Queens Road, Shanklin PO37 6AN.

Bayshore Hotel. 12-16 Pier Street, Sandown PO36 8JX. T: 01983 403154.

The Roseberry Hotel. 3 Alexandra Road, Shanklin PO37 6AF.

Two Stars

Hambledon Hotel. 11 Queens Road, Shanklin PO37 6AW. T: 01983 862403.

The Ocean Hotel. 38-40 High Street, Sandown PO36 8AB.

Eastmount Hall Hotel. 10 Eastmount Road, Shanklin PO37 6DN. T: 01983 862531.

The Harrow Lodge Hotel. 31 Palmerston Road, Shanklin PO37 6BD.

Travelodge Newport Isle of Wight. Lugley Street, Newport PO30 5HE.

Sandringham Hotel. Esplanade, Sandown PO36 8AH.

Cygnet Hotel. 58 Carter Street, Sandown PO36 8DQ.

Parkbury Hotel. 29/31 Broadway, Sandown PO36 9BB.

Royal Pier Hotel. 10 Pier Street, Sandown PO36 8JP.

Roseglen Hotel. 12 Palmerston Road, Shanklin PO37 6AS.

Medehamstede Hotel. 9 Queens Road, Shanklin PO37 6AR.

Chad Hill Hotel. 7 Hill Street, Sandown PO36 9DD.

Curraghmore Hotel. 22 Hope Road, Shanklin P037 6EA.

Malton House Hotel. 8 Park Road, Shanklin PO37 6AY.

Channel View Hotel. 4-6 Royal Street, Sandown PO36 8LP.

Holiday Parks, Hostels, and Camp Sites

Cheverton Copse Holiday Park. Scotchells Brook Lane, Sandown PO36 0JP.

Woodside Coastal Retreat. Lower Woodside Road, Wootton Bridge PO33 4JT.

Lower Hyde Holiday Park. Landguard Manor Road, Shanklin PO37 7LL.

Landguard Holiday Park. Landguard Manor Road, Shanklin PO37 7PJ.

Colwell Bay Holiday Cottages. Fort Warden Road, Colwell Bay, Freshwater.

The Orchards Holiday Caravan and Camping Park. Main Road, Newbridge, Yarmouth PO41 0TS. T: 01983 531331.

Nettlecombe Farm Holiday Cottages. Nettlecombe Lane, Whitwell PO38 2AF.

Appuldurcombe Gardens Holiday Park. Appuldurcombe Road, Wroxall, Wroxall PO38 3EP.

Old Mill Holiday Park. Mill Road, St Helens PO33 1UE. T: 01983 214117.

Whitecliff Bay Holiday Park. Hillway Road, Bembridge PO35 5PL.

Nodes Point Holiday Park. Nodes Point Holiday Park Nodes Road, St Helens PO33 1YA.

St Helens Holiday Park. Field Lane, St Helens.

Windmill Campersite. Froglands Lane, Carisbrooke PO30 3DU.

Mersley Farm Self Catering Barns and Cottages. Mersley Farm Mersley Lane, Newchurch, Sandown PO36 0NR.

The Really Green Holiday Company. Blackbridge Road, Freshwater PO40 9QJ.

Middle Barn Farm. Middle Barn Farm, Bathingbourne Lane, Sandown PO36 0LU.

Chine Farm Camping Site. Military Road, Atherfield Bay, Ventnor PO38 2JH.

Red Squirrel Glamping. Hamstead Farm, Hamstead Drive, Yarmouth PO41 0YE.

Wight Bells Camping. Newport Road, Apse Heath PO36 0JR.

Author Information

Founded in 2016, Beautiful World Escapes was established to provide reliable and up-to-date content in an authoritative manner but still draw out the magic of these locations.

Using a consistent format to provide clear information about its destinations and attractions, much of which may still be little known of, makes it easy to find what is needed. Each attraction has a genuine authenticity, giving the reader a feel for the colour and atmosphere, making each place unique. Combined with practical information, including hostels, restaurants, festivals, they also feature a handy phrasebook for getting your way around each destination and interacting with locals.

Come visit the website, Beautiful World Escapes, for more travel related guides and information.

BEAUTIFUL WORLD ESCAPES

WWW.BEAUTIFULWORLDESCAPES.COM

Printed in Great Britain
by Amazon